EYE TO EYE
with Cats

Ragdoll Cats

Lynn M. Stone

WITHDRAWN

ROURKE PUBLISHING

Vero Beach, Florida 32964

Fitchburg Public Library
5530 Lacy Road
Fitchburg, WI 53711

© 2010 Rourke Publishing LLC

All rights reserved. No part of this book may be reproduced or utilized in any form or by any means, electronic or mechanical including photocopying, recording, or by any information storage and retrieval system without permission in writing from the publisher.

www.rourkepublishing.com

PHOTO CREDITS: © Gary Martin: 18; © Eugene Bochkarev: 22; All other photos © Lynn M. Stone

Editor: Jeanne Sturm

Cover and page design by Heather Botto

Library of Congress Cataloging-in-Publication Data

Stone, Lynn M.
 Ragdoll cats / Lynn M. Stone.
    p. cm. -- (Eye to eye with cats)
 Includes index.
 ISBN 978-1-60694-338-0
 1. Ragdoll cat--Juvenile literature. I. Title.
 SF449.R34S758 2010
 636.8'3--dc22
                                            2009005989

Rourke Publishing
Printed in the United States of America, North Mankato, Minnesota
061710
061610LP-B

www.rourkepublishing.com - rourke@rourkepublishing.com
Post Office Box 643328 Vero Beach, Florida 32964

Table of Contents

3

Ragdoll Cats

The Ragdoll is a medium to large, loveable **breed** of cat. Ragdolls earned their name because of their gentle and relaxed nature. It is not true however, that a Ragdoll cat goes limp, like a doll, when it is picked up.

The Ragdoll is one of the most **affectionate** cats. It is a good thing the Ragdoll is not tiger-sized, because the Ragdoll seeks out people.

At maturity, male Ragdolls can reach 15-20 pounds (7-9 kilograms), and females 10-15 pounds (5-7 kilograms).

The Ragdoll's Looks

A Ragdoll has soft, silky fur. The breed's long fur may be any one of several color combinations. Each cat's main color, however, has darker **points**.

Points are a cat's ears, face, tail, and legs. Some Ragdoll color patterns have more color points than others.

In competition, judges look for Ragdolls with tails that are long, with a full plume.

To be eligible for championship status, a Ragdoll cat must have blue eyes and colored points. Solid-color Ragdolls can be registered, but they cannot compete.

Mitted Ragdolls have white feet in front and white boots on their back legs. They might also have a patch of white hair on their foreheads and noses.

One color pattern has no white at all. Others have large patches of white fur.

The Ragdoll has a long body with a long, bushy tail. Its round **muzzle** and full, furry cheeks give it a cuddly, doll-like expression.

A bi-color Ragdoll has a pink nose.

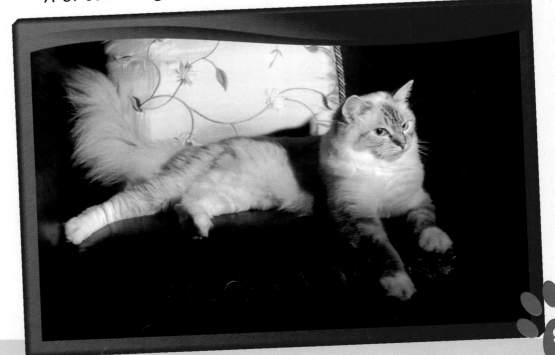

Purebred Ragdolls

A cat whose parents are both of the same breed is a purebred. The Ragdoll is one of about 40 cat breeds recognized by the Cat **Fanciers** Association.

The color points on Ragdoll kittens will darken as the cats grow up.

Most Ragdoll kittens have the same features as their mothers.

Purebred cats show the same features over and over again. A person who buys a purebred kitten can be fairly sure it will grow up to be much like its parents.

A purebred Ragdoll, for example, will have the same long body shape, dark points, and relaxed **personality** of other Ragdolls.

Like other pure breeds, Ragdolls can be expensive. Before buying one, be sure you are working with a knowledgeable **breeder**.

Kittens stay with their breeders until they are between 12 and 16 weeks old.

A Ragdoll kitten
may take two
years to fully
develop the colors
of its adult coat.

The Cat for You?

Ragdolls make wonderful companion cats. They like to be with and on people. They can be trained to walk on a leash. Many Ragdolls follow their owners around, earning the breed the nickname puppy cats.

Although Radgolls can be leash-trained, it is still a good idea to keep them inside where they are out of harm's way.

Regular grooming helps keep a Ragdoll's fur free from tangles, and cats like the comb's touch.

Ragdolls are good with children, other cats, and dogs. They require only weekly **grooming** with a metal comb.

Ragdolls are playful, but not to the extreme. Because of their gentle nature, they are not likely to scratch their human handlers.

Ragdolls are best kept indoors. Their gentleness can be a problem outdoors, where they may not defend themselves against other animals.

Ragdolls respond well to children and other pets.

Ragdolls mature slowly. Their coat color is fully developed at two years, and they reach full size and weight at four.

The History of Ragdolls

Ann Baker of Riverside, California, began the Ragdoll breed in the 1960s. Her work with Ragdolls was later taken up by Denny and Laura Dayton.

Birman

White Persian

The Ragdoll's immediate ancestors were probably not purebred cats, but no one knows for sure. Ann Baker chose as the father a pointed male that was a **Birman** cat look-alike. The longhaired female, Josephine, was a white **Persian** or **Angora** type.

These cats and their offspring produced remarkably **docile** kittens. Breeders worked to keep the cats' sweet nature by carefully choosing new parent cats for several years.

By the 1990s, the Ragdoll was a successful new breed. Today it is the third most popular longhaired purebred cat after the Persian and Maine Coon.

Bi-color Ragdolls have a triangle-shaped patch of white fur on their faces.

ABOUT CAT BREEDS

The beginnings of domestic, or tame, cats date back at least 8,000 years, when people began to raise the kittens of small wild cats. By 4,000 years ago, the Egyptians had totally tame, household cats. Most actual breeds of cats, however, are fewer than 150 years old. People created breeds by selecting parent cats that had certain qualities people liked and wanted to repeat. Two longhaired parents, for example, were likely to produce longhaired kittens. By carefully choosing cat parents, cat fanciers have managed to create cats with predictable qualities—breeds.

Ragdoll Cat Facts

- 🐾 Date of Origin – 1960s

- 🐾 Place of Origin – United States

- 🐾 Overall Size – medium to large

- 🐾 Weight – 10-20 pounds (4.5-9 kilograms)

- 🐾 Coat – medium long

- 🐾 Grooming – once weekly

- 🐾 Activity Level – fairly low

- 🐾 **Temperament** – very affectionate, relaxed

- 🐾 Voice – quiet

Glossary

affectionate (uh-FEK-shuh-nuht): loving

Angora (an-GOR-uh): an ancient, longhaired breed of Turkish cat named for the the capitol city

Birman (BURR-min): a pointed, Burmese cat breed that looks like a large bodied Siamese

breed (BREED): a particular kind of domestic animal, such as a Ragdoll cat

breeder (BREED-er): someone who matches animal parents and raises their young

docile (DOSS-uhl): calm and easy to train or control

fanciers (FAN-see-erz): those who raise and work to improve purebred cats

grooming (GROOM-ing): the act of brushing, combing, and cleaning

muzzle (MUHZ-uhl): an animal's nose, mouth, and jaws; its face

Persian (PURR-zhun): a popular longhaired breed of cat with a flat face

personality (pur-suh-NAL-uh-tee): the qualities and behavior that make one person or animal different from others

points (POINTS): an animal's ears, face, tail, and legs

temperament (TEM-pur-uh-muhnt): an animal's nature or personality

Index

Websites to Visit

kids.cfa.org

www.rfci.org

www.ticaeo.com

About the Author

A former teacher and sports writer, Lynn Stone is a widely published children's book author and nature photographer. He has photographed animals on all seven continents. The National Science Teachers Association chose one of his books, *Box Turtles*, as an Outstanding Science Trade Book for 2008. Stone, who grew up in Connecticut, lives in northern Illinois with his wife, golden retriever, two cats, and abundant fishing tackle.